When No One is Clapping for You, You Must Clap for Yourself

Katie Rose

Published by Katie Rose, 2024.

While every precaution has been taken in the preparation of this book, the publisher assumes no responsibility for errors or omissions, or for damages resulting from the use of the information contained herein.

WHEN NO ONE IS CLAPPING FOR YOU, YOU MUST CLAP FOR YOURSELF

First edition. May 2, 2024.

Copyright © 2024 Katie Rose.

ISBN: 979-8224638161

Written by Katie Rose.

Embracing your inner strength begins with acknowledging that you are a force to be reckoned with, armed with the potential to achieve greatness. Inner strength is not a short-term thing but rather a muscle that can be sculpted and strengthened through consistent long-term practice. It necessitates a commitment to self-improvement and a willingness to step into the unknown. Like a blacksmith forging steel, you must expose yourself to the flames of challenge, overcoming them one by one.

Embracing your inner strength means extending grace and understanding to yourself in times of vulnerability and perceived weakness. Acknowledging that imperfection is part of the human experience. You need to grant yourself permission to stumble and falter, learning valuable lessons from these moments. It is through vulnerability that the most authentic self appears, forging connections between you and others around you.

By sharing the raw, genuine moments of vulnerability you experience along the way, you give others permission to embrace their own struggles and persevere. Encouraging others to unearth themselves creates a ripple effect that goes beyond personal achievement and enriches the world around you.

So, take that step of discomfort and share yourself with others. You've got this baby!

Katie Rose

A Guide to Building Self-esteem for Loners

Chapter 1: Understanding Loneliness

The Nature of Loneliness

Loneliness is a universal human experience that can affect anyone, regardless of their circumstances. It is a feeling of isolation and disconnection from others, which can lead to feelings of sadness, emptiness, and despair. For many loners, this feeling of being alone can be overwhelming and difficult to overcome. However, it is important to understand that loneliness is a natural emotion that everyone experiences at some point in their lives.

Loneliness is a universal human experience that can affect anyone, regardless of the circumstances. It entails a sense of isolation and disconnection from others, leading to feelings of sadness, emptiness, and depression. For many individuals who experience loneliness, this sensation of solitude can be overwhelming and challenging to overcome. However, it's crucial to recognize that loneliness is a natural emotion that everyone encounters at some point in their lives.

Loneliness doesn't just affect emotional well-being but can also have significant implications for physical health. Research shows that chronic loneliness is linked to a higher risk of cardiovascular diseases, weakened immune systems, and premature death.

Despite the technological interconnectedness of the modern era, feelings of loneliness have paradoxically intensified for many individuals. Social media platforms, while offering avenues for communication, often foster superficial connections and a sense of comparison that worsens isolation.

Life transitions such as moving to a new city, experiencing the loss of a loved one, or retiring can amplify feelings of loneliness due to significant changes in social networks. Despite the reputation surrounding loneliness, it's essential to acknowledge it as a legitimate human experience. Seeking support from friends, family, or mental health professionals, engaging in meaningful activities, and developing self-compassion are important steps in addressing and coping with loneliness. Also, volunteering, joining clubs or interest groups, and taking part in community events can c connections and alleviate feelings of isolation.

Accepting loneliness as part of the human experience can lead to a deeper understanding of yourself and clear the way for meaningful connections with others.

The nature of loneliness is indeed intricate and multifaceted, stemming from various factors that encompass both internal and external influences. Social isolation, characterized by a lack of regular interaction or meaningful connections with others, is a primary contributor to feelings of loneliness. The absence of deep and fulfilling relationships, whether romantic, platonic, or familial, can worsen this sense of isolation. Low self-esteem and negative self-perception can perpetuate loneliness by hindering individuals from forming and keeping meaningful connections due to feelings of unworthiness or inadequacy.

Transitions in life can trigger or intensify feelings of loneliness. Relocating to a new city or starting a new job, for instance, can disrupt established social networks, leaving individuals without the familiar support systems they once had. This disruption can evoke feelings of disconnection and alienation, contributing to a heightened sense of loneliness.

Understanding the intricate interplay of these factors is pivotal in effectively addressing and overcoming loneliness. By recognizing the root causes, individuals can take proactive steps to cultivate meaningful connections, bolster self-esteem, and get through life transitions more smoothly. Strategies such as actively seeking out social opportunities, engaging in activities that foster genuine connections, and practicing self-care and self-compassion can help individuals mitigate feelings of loneliness and cultivate a sense of belonging and fulfillment in their lives.

For many loners who prefer solitude, the nature of loneliness can be significantly influenced by societal stigma and misconceptions surrounding solitude. Society often associates being alone with experiencing loneliness, overlooking the possibility of finding fulfillment and contentment in one's own company. Consequently, individuals who choose solitude over constant social interaction may encounter societal pressures to conform to norms and expectations, leading to heightened feelings of isolation and loneliness.

These pressures can be particularly pronounced for introverted individuals or those who thrive in solitary activities. It's imperative for individuals who relate with solitude to challenge these societal beliefs and embrace their unique qualities and strengths. By recognizing the distinction between solitude and loneliness, individuals can assert their true self and cultivate a deeper understanding of their own needs and preferences, creating a sense of contentment in their solitude.

One effective strategy for combating loneliness is to focus on building self-esteem and confidence from within. Developing a positive self-image and prioritizing self-care are vital steps that individuals, including loners, can take to enhance their mental and emotional well-being. By developing a strong sense of self-worth and belonging, individuals can ease feelings of isolation and build a deeper connection with themselves and others.

Engaging in activities that bring joy and fulfillment, such as hobbies, exercise, and creative pursuits, not only provide a sense of purpose but also serve as avenues for self-expression and personal growth. These activities offer opportunities for individuals to connect with like-minded individuals and build supportive social networks, reducing feelings of loneliness and enhancing overall life satisfaction.

Practicing mindfulness and self-compassion can help individuals handle moments of solitude with greater ease, building the ability to last and inner peace during the challenges of loneliness. By nurturing a positive relationship with oneself, individuals can develop the confidence and power needed to understand the feelings of loneliness and thrive in their individual journey of self-discovery and personal growth.

Understanding the intricate dynamics of loneliness is important for loners beginning a journey to build their self-esteem and confidence. By reaching into the nature of loneliness and recognizing the different factors that contribute to feelings of isolation and disconnection, individuals can take proactive steps to address these issues and create a greater sense of belonging and fulfillment in their lives. In addition to self-awareness, applying effective self-care practices is important in nurturing mental and emotional well-being. This may include prioritizing activities that promote relaxation, such as mindfulness exercises, journaling, or spending time in nature.

Practicing self-acceptance and learning positive self-talk can significantly affect your belief of yourself and your place in the world. By challenging negative thought patterns and embracing their unique qualities and strengths, loners can gradually overcome feelings of loneliness and build a solid foundation for personal growth.

It's important to recognize that seeking support is a sign of strength, not weakness. Loners are not alone in their struggles, and there are numerous resources and communities available to provide guidance and encouragement along their journey towards self-confidence and empowerment. Whether it's reaching out to friends, family, or mental health professionals, or seeking help in online forums and support groups, there is always help and support available for those who are willing to take the first step towards positive change.

Remember, building self-esteem and confidence is a process that takes time and patience, but with determination and support, loners can embark on an exciting journey towards greater self-awareness, strength, and fulfillment.

Effects of Loneliness on Mental Health

Loneliness can have a significant impact on mental health, particularly among individuals who identify as loners or find themselves experiencing prolonged periods of solitude. The ramifications of loneliness go far beyond mere emotional discomfort, encompassing a spectrum of adverse effects that can detrimentally affect one's psychological well-being. Among these effects are heightened levels of anxiety and depression, which often go with prolonged feelings of isolation. Moreover, loneliness can erode overall mental well-being, leading to a diminished sense of purpose, satisfaction, and fulfillment in life.

Recognizing and addressing the impact of loneliness is important for safeguarding mental and emotional health. Individuals in this situation must proactively acknowledge and confront the effects of loneliness to prevent further deterioration of their well-being. This may involve seeking professional support from therapists or counselors trained in addressing loneliness and its associated mental health challenges. Additionally, adopting coping strategies such as mindfulness practices, self-care rituals, and engaging in fulfilling activities can serve as effective means of fending off the negative effects of loneliness on mental health.

Creating meaningful connections with others, even for individuals who predominantly identify as loners, can play a vital role in alleviating feelings of isolation and bolstering mental strength. This can be achieved through participation in social groups, volunteering opportunities, or online communities centered around shared interests. By nurturing authentic connections and building a support network, individuals can feel a sense of belonging and fortify their mental and emotional well-being in the face of loneliness. Prioritizing mental health and taking proactive steps to address the effects of loneliness are essential for maintaining a healthy mind and spirit during periods of solitude.

Loneliness often correlates with heightened levels of anxiety, representing one of the most prevalent effects on mental health. The experience of isolation or disconnection from others can trigger a cascade of negative thought patterns, worsening feelings of apprehension and distress. Individuals grappling with loneliness may find themselves filled by racing thoughts, accompanied by physical manifestations such as an accelerated heart rate or perspiration, intensifying the overall sense of unease. Recognizing the interconnectedness of loneliness and anxiety underscores the importance of using effective coping mechanisms to manage these distressing emotions.

In addition to traditional coping strategies such as deep breathing exercises and mindfulness practices, individuals can explore a variety of holistic approaches to help alleviate anxiety. Incorporating regular physical activity into one's routine, for instance, has been shown to release endorphins and reduce symptoms of anxiety. Maintaining a balanced diet rich in nutrients can support overall mental well-being and provide the necessary foundation for managing anxiety. And seeking professional guidance from therapists or counselors proficient in cognitive-behavioral techniques can equip individuals with invaluable tools to challenge negative thought patterns and build fortitude in the face of loneliness-induced anxiety.

Fostering connections with others, even in small ways, can serve as a potent antidote to loneliness-induced anxiety. Engaging in meaningful conversations, taking part in group activities, or volunteering within the community can provide opportunities for social interaction and emotional support, helping to get rid of feelings of isolation and reducing anxiety levels. By actively nurturing connections and prioritizing self-care practices, individuals can effectively manage the adverse effects of loneliness on mental health and cultivate a greater sense of well-being in their lives.

Depression is another common effect of loneliness on mental health. The absence of social connections or meaningful relationships can lead to feelings of despair and hopelessness taking root. This emotional state often appears as a profound lack of motivation, making even once-pleasurable activities feel meaningless. Individuals grappling with loneliness-induced depression may experience a deep sense of sadness that affects various aspects of their lives.

Recognizing the detrimental impact of loneliness on mental health underscores the importance of seeking professional support. Therapists or counselors skilled in addressing depression can offer invaluable guidance and help in understanding these complex emotions. Through therapy, individuals can explore the underlying causes of their loneliness and depression, find negative thought patterns, and develop coping strategies tailored to their unique needs.

In addition to seeking professional help, individuals can also take proactive steps to manage loneliness-induced depression through self-care practices and lifestyle modifications. Engaging in regular physical activity, maintaining a healthy diet, and prioritizing adequate sleep can contribute to improved mood and overall well-being. Forming meaningful connections with others, whether through social activities, support groups, or volunteer work, can provide a vital source of emotional support and alleviate feelings of isolation.

Exploring creative outlets and hobbies can serve as a therapeutic means of self-expression and distraction from depressive symptoms. Activities such as art, music, or journaling offer opportunities for individuals to channel their emotions constructively and foster a sense of purpose and fulfillment. By embracing a holistic approach to managing loneliness-induced depression, individuals can reclaim their mental health and rebuild themselves in the face of adversity.

Loneliness can also have a significant impact on overall well-being. When we are isolated, we may neglect our physical health, engage in unhealthy coping mechanisms such as substance abuse or overeating, and have difficulty keeping a balanced lifestyle. It is important for loners or those feeling alone to prioritize self-care practices such as exercise, healthy eating, and adequate sleep in order to maintain a sense of well-being in the face of loneliness.

The effects of loneliness on mental health can be profound for individuals who identify as loners or are feeling alone. It is important for these individuals to recognize and address these effects in order to maintain a healthy mind and spirit. By seeking support from a therapist or counselor, developing healthy coping mechanisms for anxiety and depression, and prioritizing self-care practices, individuals can face the challenges of loneliness and build a strong sense of self- esteem and confidence from within.

Common Causes of Loneliness

One common cause of loneliness is a lack of social connections. Loners often struggle to build and keep meaningful relationships with others, leading to feelings of isolation and alienation. Without a strong support system in place, it can be difficult to combat feelings of loneliness and build self-esteem. This is why it is important for loners to actively work on building their social skills and connecting with others who share similar interests and values.

Another common cause of loneliness is low self-esteem. When individuals do not feel confident in themselves or their abilities, they may struggle to put themselves out there and make new connections. This can lead to a cycle of isolation and loneliness, as individuals may feel unworthy of forming relationships with others. Building self-esteem is crucial for combatting loneliness, as it allows individuals to feel more comfortable in their own skin and confidently reach out to others.

Additionally, past traumas or negative experiences can contribute to feelings of loneliness. Loners may have experienced rejection, abandonment, or other forms of emotional pain that have left them feeling distrustful of others. These past wounds can make it challenging to open up and form close connections with others, leading to feelings of loneliness and isolation. Working through these past traumas with a therapist or counselor can help individuals heal and move forward in their quest for connection and belonging.

Now, societal pressures and expectations can also contribute to feelings of loneliness. Loners may feel pressure to conform to societal norms and expectations, which can lead to feelings of inadequacy and isolation. It is important for individuals to recognize and challenge these societal pressures, and to embrace their uniqueness and individuality. By accepting and celebrating their true selves, loners can build confidence and self-esteem, and attract others who appreciate them for who they are.

Loneliness can stem from a variety of sources, including a lack of social connections, low self-esteem, past traumas, and societal pressures. It is important for loners to address these underlying causes and work on building their self-esteem and social skills to be able to combat feelings of loneliness. By reaching out to others, working through past traumas, and embracing their true selves, loners can build confidence and form meaningful connections with others. With the right support and guidance, loners can overcome feelings of loneliness and build a strong sense of self-worth and belonging.

A Guide to Building Self-esteem for Loners

Chapter 2: The Power of Self-Esteem

Defining Self-Esteem

Self-esteem is a crucial aspect of our overall well-being, yet it is often misunderstood or overlooked, especially by those who identify as loners or who feel alone. In this chapter, we will explore the true meaning of self-esteem and its importance in building confidence from within.

Self-esteem can be defined as the overall opinion we have of ourselves, it is how we value ourselves and perceive our worth. For loners or individuals who feel alone, self-esteem can be particularly challenging to cultivate, as external validation and social interactions may be limited. However, it is essential to remember that self-esteem comes from within and is not dependent on others opinions or approval.

Having a healthy level of self-esteem is crucial for our mental, emotional, and physical well-being. It affects how we think, feel, and behave in various situations, and it plays a significant role in our ability to cope with challenges and setbacks. For loners or individuals feeling alone, building self-esteem can provide a sense of inner strength and perseverance to face life's ups and downs with confidence and grace.

Self-esteem is not about being arrogant or egotistical, it is about recognizing and appreciating our own worth and capabilities. It is about acknowledging our strengths and weaknesses, accepting ourselves as we are, and striving to become the best version of ourselves. For loners or individuals feeling alone, developing a healthy sense of self-esteem can be a transformative journey towards self-acceptance and self-love.

In the following chapters, we will dive deeper into practical strategies and exercises to help you build self-esteem and confidence from within. By understanding the true essence of self-esteem and its importance in our lives, we can empower ourselves to accept our uniqueness, connect with our inner strength, and thrive as individuals, even in moments of solitude. Remember, true confidence comes from within, and by nurturing your self-esteem, you can unlock your full potential and live a fulfilling and authentic life.

Importance of Self-Esteem in Building Confidence

In the journey of building self-esteem, one key part that cannot be overlooked is the importance of self-esteem in building confidence. Self-esteem serves as the foundation upon which confidence is built, allowing individuals to believe in their own abilities and worthiness.

When individuals have a strong sense of self-esteem, they are better equipped to face challenges and setbacks with a positive mindset. This inner strength and belief in oneself are essential in overcoming the feelings of loneliness and isolation that loners may experience. By recognizing your own value and self-worth, you can begin to break free from the cycle of negative self-talk and self-doubt that often plagues those who feel alone.

Self-esteem plays a crucial role in shaping how individuals perceive themselves and their place in the world. When individuals have a healthy sense of self-worth, they are more likely to engage in positive self-care practices and set boundaries that prioritize their well-being. This, in turn, leads to increased feelings of confidence and self-assurance, allowing loners to step out of their comfort zones and connect with others in meaningful ways.

For those seeking guidance in building their self-esteem and confidence, it is important to recognize that these qualities are interconnected and rely on one another for growth. By focusing on achieving a positive self-image and practicing self- compassion, loners can begin to build the confidence needed to thrive in their personal and professional lives. Through the support and guidance of life coaching, health and wellness coaching, and confidence building coaching, individuals can develop the tools and strategies necessary to boost their self-esteem and grasp their inner strength.

The importance of self-esteem in building confidence cannot be understated for loners and those feeling alone. By fostering a sense of self-worth and self-belief, individuals can unlock their full potential and grab on to the opportunities that come their way. With the right support and guidance, individuals can begin a journey of self-discovery and find the confidence to travel the world with grace and strength.

Ways to Improve Self-Esteem

We will now explore various strategies and techniques that loners and individuals feeling alone can implement to boost their self-esteem and confidence. Building self-esteem is essential for overall well-being and happiness, and it is especially important for loners who may struggle with feelings of isolation and inadequacy. By incorporating these tips into your daily routine, you can start to cultivate a positive self-image and love your unique qualities.

One way to improve self-esteem is to practice self-care and prioritize your physical and mental well-being. This includes eating nutritious foods, getting regular exercise, and engaging in activities that bring you joy and relaxation. Taking care of yourself both physically and emotionally can help you feel more confident and empowered in your own skin.

Another effective way to boost self-esteem is to challenge negative thoughts and beliefs about yourself. Loners often struggle with self-doubt and self-criticism, which can erode their confidence over time. By learning to find and reframe these negative thoughts, you can begin to cultivate a more positive and compassionate inner dialogue.

Setting achievable goals and celebrating your accomplishments, no matter how small, can also help improve self-esteem. Loners may feel overwhelmed by the idea of setting goals but breaking them down into manageable steps can make them more attainable. By acknowledging your progress and rewarding yourself for your efforts, you can build momentum and confidence in your abilities.

Building a support network of friends, family members, or mentors can also be instrumental in improving self-esteem. Loners may feel hesitant to reach out for help, but having a strong support system can provide encouragement, guidance, and reassurance during challenging times. Surrounding yourself with positive and supportive individuals can help you see your own worth and potential more clearly.

And lastly, practicing self-compassion and acceptance is crucial for improving self-esteem. Loners may be particularly hard on themselves, but learning to treat yourself with kindness and understanding can foster a sense of inner peace and confidence. By embracing your flaws and imperfections as part of what makes you unique, you can begin to cultivate a more positive self-image and build lasting self-esteem.

A Guide to Building Self-esteem for Loners

Chapter 3: Building Confidence from Within

Identifying Your Strengths and Weaknesses

To build self-esteem and confidence, it is important to first identify your strengths and weaknesses. This self- awareness is crucial for loners and those feeling alone, as it can help you understand yourself better and make positive changes in your life. By recognizing your strengths, you can build on them and use them to your advantage. Similarly, acknowledging your weaknesses allows you to work on improving them and becoming a better version of yourself.

One way to find your strengths is to reflect on past accomplishments and successes. Think about times when you felt proud of yourself or received positive feedback from others. These moments can help you pinpoint your unique abilities and talents. Additionally, consider what activities bring you joy and fulfillment, as these are often indicators of your strengths. By focusing on your strengths, you can boost your self-confidence and feel more empowered in your daily life.

On the other hand, it is equally important to identify your weaknesses in order to address areas for improvement. Reflect on situations where you may have struggled or received negative feedback. This can help you find patterns or habits that may be holding you back. By acknowledging your weaknesses, you can take steps to overcome them and grow as an individual. Remember, everyone has weaknesses, and it is okay to ask for help or seek support when needed.

A life coach, health and wellness coach, or confidence building coach can help individuals identify their strengths and weaknesses. They can encourage you to engage in self-reflection and introspection to gain a better understanding of yourself. They can provide you with tools and resources to assess your skills and abilities and guide you in setting goals for personal growth and development. By helping you identify your strengths and weaknesses, they can support you in building your self-esteem and confidence.

A Guide to Building Self-esteem for Loners

Identifying your strengths and weaknesses is a crucial step in building self-esteem and confidence. For loners and those feeling alone, this self-awareness can be transformative in helping you understand yourself better and make positive changes in your life. It is important to accept this process in your journey towards personal growth and empowerment. By recognizing and embracing both your strengths and weaknesses, you can cultivate a greater sense of self- worth and confidence from within.

Setting Realistic Goals

Setting realistic goals is an essential step in building self-esteem and confidence, especially for loners and individuals who may be feeling alone. It is important to understand that setting goals that are too lofty or unattainable can lead to feelings of failure and inadequacy. By setting realistic goals, you are setting yourself up for success and creating a sense of accomplishment that can boost your self-esteem.

When setting goals, it is important to be specific and measurable. Instead of setting a vague goal like "I want to be more confident," try setting a specific goal like "I will attend a social event and introduce myself to at least three new people." This way, you have a clear target to work towards and can measure your progress along the way. Setting measurable goals allows you to track your achievements and celebrate your successes, no matter how small they may seem.

It is also important to set goals that are achievable within a reasonable timeframe. If you set a goal that is too ambitious or unrealistic, you may become discouraged and give up before you even get started. Start small and gradually work your way up to bigger goals as you gain confidence and momentum. By setting achievable goals, you are setting yourself up for success and building your self-esteem in the process.

Another important aspect of setting realistic goals is to make sure they are relevant to your overall well-being and happiness. Take time to reflect on what truly matters to you and what will bring you the most fulfillment. Setting goals that align with your values and priorities will give you a sense of purpose and motivation to keep pushing forward, even when faced with challenges or setbacks.

Setting realistic goals serves as a cornerstone in our journey of building self-esteem and confidence, particularly for loners or individuals living in periods of solitude. These goals provide a sense of direction and purpose, serving as guiding beacons towards personal growth and fulfillment. When crafting goals, it's essential to adhere to the SMART criteria: Specific, Measurable, Achievable, Relevant, and Time-bound. By delineating clear and precise goals, individuals can set up a roadmap for success and keep focus during the challenges of loneliness.

Specificity entails defining goals with clarity and precision, outlining the desired outcomes and the steps needed to achieve them. Measurability involves quantifying progress and success criteria, enabling individuals to track their achievements and adjust their efforts accordingly. Ensuring goals are achievable involves setting realistic expectations and acknowledging personal strengths and limitations. Relevance needs aligning goals with your values, interests, and long-term dreams, ensuring they resonate deeply with you. Establishing a timeframe for goal achievement instills a sense of urgency and accountability, motivating you to take consistent action towards your objectives.

Remember to celebrate your achievements along the way and be kind to yourself, even when things don't go as planned. With dedication and perseverance, you can achieve your goals and build the confidence you deserve.

Overcoming Negative Self-Talk

Overcoming negative self-talk is a crucial step in building self-esteem and confidence for loners and those who often feel alone. Negative self-talk can be incredibly damaging, as it reinforces feelings of inadequacy and worthlessness. By learning to identify and challenge these negative thoughts, you can begin to build a more positive inner dialogue.

One of the key strategies for overcoming negative self-talk is mindfulness. Mindfulness involves paying attention to your thoughts and feelings without judgment. By practicing mindfulness, you can become more aware of when negative self-talk arises and begin to challenge these thoughts. This can help you develop a more compassionate and understanding relationship with yourself.

Another important technique for overcoming negative self-talk is cognitive behavioral therapy (CBT). CBT helps you identify and challenge negative thought patterns that contribute to low self-esteem. By working with a therapist or coach, you can learn to reframe negative thoughts and beliefs, replacing them with more positive ones. This can help you build confidence and self-esteem over time.

In addition to setting realistic goals, surrounding oneself with positive influences and supportive individuals is paramount in the journey of building self-esteem and confidence. While loners and individuals experiencing periods of solitude may find it challenging to cultivate a supportive social network, actively seeking out positive relationships is essential for bolstering self-esteem.

Seeking friendships and relationships that uplift and inspire can provide a source of encouragement and validation, creating a sense of belonging and acceptance. These connections offer opportunities for mutual support and growth, enabling people to thrive in a nurturing environment. Whether through shared interests, values, or experiences, creating meaningful connections with like-minded individuals can cultivate a friendship and a sense of empowerment.

Remember that building self-esteem is a journey, not a destination. It takes time and effort to overcome negative self-talk and build confidence from within. Be patient with yourself and celebrate small victories along the way. With dedication and support, you can learn to silence your inner critic and take on a more positive mindset.

A Guide to Building Self-esteem for Loners

Chapter 4: Building Positive Relationships

Finding Your Tribe

One of the biggest challenges faced by loners and people feeling alone is the lack of a supportive community. In a world that often values extroversion and social connections, it can be difficult for introverted individuals to find their place. However, it is essential for loners to understand that they are not alone in their feelings of isolation. There are others out there who share similar experiences and struggles, and it is important to find your tribe, a group of like-minded individuals who understand and support you.

Finding your tribe is about connecting with people who share your values, interests, and beliefs. These are the people who will lift you up when you are feeling down, celebrate your successes, and provide a sense of belonging and acceptance. It may take time and effort to find your tribe, but the rewards are well worth it. Surrounding yourself with positive and supportive individuals can have a profound impact on your self-esteem and overall well-being.

Life coaching, health and wellness coaching, and confidence building coaching can all play a role in helping loners find their tribe. A life coach can help you find your values and interests and guide you in connecting with others who share similar passions. A health and wellness coach can support you in developing healthy habits and routines that will help you feel more confident and energized. And a confidence building coach can provide you with the tools and techniques to overcome your fears and step out of your comfort zone to meet new people.

It is important for loners to remember that finding your tribe is not about changing who you are or pretending to be someone you're not. It is about embracing your unique qualities and finding people who appreciate and celebrate them. Your tribe should be a safe space where you can be yourself without judgment or criticism. By surrounding yourself with people who understand and support you, you will be able to build your self-esteem and confidence from within.

Finding your tribe is a crucial step in building self-esteem for loners. It is about connecting with like-minded individuals who share your values and interests, and who can provide you with the support and encouragement you need to thrive. Life coaching, health and wellness coaching, and confidence building coaching can all help you in this journey, providing you with the guidance and tools necessary to find your tribe and create a sense of belonging and acceptance.

Remember, you are not alone, there are others out there who understand and support you. Accept your uniqueness, connect with your tribe, and watch your self-esteem soar.

Nurturing Healthy Relationships

Building and keeping healthy relationships is essential for our well-being, especially for those of us who may identify as loners or feel alone at times. Nurturing healthy relationships can help us feel supported, connected, and valued in our lives. In this subchapter, we will explore key strategies for fostering and sustaining positive relationships with others.

One important aspect of nurturing healthy relationships is communication. Effective communication involves actively listening to others, expressing our thoughts and feelings honestly, and being open to feedback. By improving our communication skills, we can deepen our connections with others and build trust and understanding in our relationships.

Creating and keeping boundaries is crucial for fostering healthy relationships. Boundaries help define limits and expectations in interpersonal interactions, protecting one's well-being and values. By clearly communicating boundaries, individuals assert their autonomy and express their needs and preferences, nurturing mutual respect and understanding in relationships.

Setting boundaries acts as a shield against potential harm or exploitation, helping individuals to keep control in their lives. Whether it's defining emotional boundaries to ward off manipulation or establishing physical boundaries to preserve personal space and independence, creating clear limits is vital for maintaining mental and emotional well-being.

Creating self-awareness and self-compassion is important to setting and enforcing boundaries effectively. By understanding one's own needs, values, and limits, individuals can set up boundaries that align with their authentic selves and promote well-being. Practicing self-compassion allows individuals to prioritize their own needs without guilt or self-judgment, fostering healthier relationships based on mutual respect and reciprocity.

Building trust is also crucial in nurturing healthy relationships. Trust is the foundation of any strong relationship, and it is important to be reliable, honest, and consistent in our interactions with others. By showing trustworthiness and being trustworthy ourselves, we can cultivate trust in our relationships and deepen our connections with others.

In addition to communication, boundaries, and trust, it is important to practice empathy and compassion in our relationships. By empathizing with others, putting ourselves in their shoes, and showing compassion and understanding, we can strengthen our relationships and create a supportive and caring environment for ourselves and those around us. Nurturing healthy relationships takes time, effort, and commitment, but the rewards of feeling connected, valued, and supported are well worth it.

Setting Boundaries

Setting boundaries is a crucial aspect of building self-esteem, especially for loners and those who often feel alone. It involves defining what is acceptable and unacceptable in your relationships and interactions with others. By setting boundaries, you are protecting your mental and emotional well-being, while also showing respect for yourself. It is important to remember that boundaries are not meant to push people away, but rather to create healthy and sustainable connections with others.

As a loner, you may find it challenging to set boundaries, as you may fear rejection or conflict. However, it is essential to prioritize your own needs and feelings in order to build confidence and self-esteem. Setting boundaries can help you feel more in control of your life and relationships, leading to a greater sense of empowerment and self-worth. Remember that it is okay to say no and assert your needs and desires in a respectful manner.

When setting boundaries, it is important to communicate them clearly and assertively. Be honest with yourself about what you are comfortable with and what crosses the line for you. Practice saying no without feeling guilty or ashamed, as your feelings and needs are just as valid as anyone else's. By setting boundaries, you are showing others how you expect to be treated, which can lead to more fulfilling and respectful relationships.

Setting boundaries is not only done by defining personal limits but also recognizing and addressing instances where those boundaries are not respected by others. It's essential to be attuned to situations where individuals overstep or disregard your boundaries, as this can compromise your well-being and autonomy. When faced with boundary violations, it's important to respond assertively yet calmly, clearly communicating your discomfort and reinforcing your limits. Remember, prioritizing your own well-being is not selfish, it's a fundamental aspect of self-care.

It's essential to recognize that setting boundaries may entail letting go of relationships that consistently disregard or undermine your well-being. While this can be a challenging process, prioritizing your mental and emotional health is important. By releasing toxic relationships and surrounding yourself with supportive individuals, you create space for personal growth and positive experiences.

Setting boundaries is an essential part of building self-esteem and confidence for loners and those feeling alone. By defining what is acceptable and unacceptable in your relationships, you are prioritizing your own well-being and showing respect for yourself. Remember that it is okay to say no and assert your needs, as this will lead to healthier and more fulfilling connections with others. Stay true to yourself and your boundaries and watch as your confidence and self- esteem grow.

———

Trust yourself to honor your needs and feelings, and don't hesitate to assertively assert your boundaries when necessary. Remember that boundaries are not rigid structures but flexible guidelines that evolve with your growth and self-discovery. By creating a strong sense of self-respect and boundary-setting skills, you empower yourself to build relationships with confidence and authenticity.

A Guide to Building Self-esteem for Loners

Chapter 5: Self-Care and Wellness

Importance of Self-Care for Loners

Loners, people feeling alone, often find solace in their own company. While spending time alone can be peaceful and rejuvenating, it is important for loners to prioritize self-care in order to maintain their mental, emotional, and physical well-being. We will explore the importance of self-care for loners and how it can help them build confidence from within.

Self-care for loners is essential because it allows them to recharge and refuel their energy levels. Loners often spend a lot of time in their own thoughts, which can be draining. By taking the time to practice self-care activities such as meditation, journaling, or simply taking a walk in nature, loners can rejuvenate their minds and bodies, leading to increased feelings of well-being and confidence.

Self-care for loners can help them set up a sense of routine and structure in their lives. Loners may struggle with feelings of isolation and loneliness, but by incorporating self-care practices into their daily routines, they can create a sense of stability and consistency. This can help them feel more grounded and in control of their lives, leading to increased feelings of self-worth and confidence.

Self-care for loners also plays a crucial role in fostering self-compassion and self-love. Loners may be prone to negative self-talk and feelings of self-doubt, but by practicing self-care activities that promote self-compassion, such as positive affirmations or self-care rituals, they can learn to treat themselves with kindness and understanding. This can help them build a stronger sense of self-esteem and confidence in their abilities.

Self-care is a fundamental aspect of building self-esteem and confidence, especially for individuals who like solitude or identify as loners. Giving priority to self-care practices that address mental, emotional, and physical well-being is vital for creating a robust sense of self.

It's essential to recognize that self-care is not selfish but rather a necessary investment in one's well-being and happiness. By prioritizing self-care, loners can build a strong foundation of self-esteem and confidence, encouraging them to face life's ups and downs with grit and grace. Remember, taking care of yourself is not only beneficial for your own well-being but also enables you to show up more fully for others and contribute positively to the world around you.

Remember, taking care of yourself is not selfish, it is necessary for your well-being and happiness.

Mindfulness and Meditation Practices

Let's explore the powerful connection between mindfulness and meditation practices and how they can greatly benefit loners and those who are feeling alone. Loneliness can often lead to negative self-talk and low self- esteem, but by incorporating mindfulness and meditation into your daily routine, you can begin to cultivate a more positive mindset and build confidence from within.

Mindfulness, often described as the art of being present in the moment, involves achieving a non-judgmental awareness of one's thoughts, emotions, and environment. This practice is particularly valuable for individual's experiencing loneliness, as it offers a tool for overcoming negative thought patterns and creating a greater sense of inner peace and strength. When loneliness sets in, it's common to be inundated with self-critical thoughts and rumination about one's circumstances.

By incorporating mindfulness techniques into daily life, individuals can develop the ability to see these thoughts without becoming entangled in them. Through mindfulness, individuals can cultivate a sense of detachment from their negative self-talk, allowing them to approach their thoughts with curiosity and compassion rather than judgment.

Mindfulness practices such as deep breathing exercises, body and mind scans, or mindful walking can help individuals anchor themselves in the present moment, fostering a greater sense of calm and contentment amidst feelings of loneliness.

Meditation, on the other hand, is a practice of focusing your mind and calming your thoughts. Loners and those feeling alone can benefit greatly from meditation, as it provides a sense of peace and calm in the midst of loneliness. By taking time each day to sit quietly and focus on your breath or a mantra, you can begin to quiet the negative chatter in your mind and cultivate a sense of inner peace and self-assurance.

By incorporating mindfulness and meditation practices into your daily routine, you can begin to build a strong foundation of self-esteem and confidence from within. These practices can help you become more aware of your thoughts and feelings, allowing you to challenge negative self-talk and cultivate a more positive outlook on life. As you continue to practice mindfulness and meditation, you will begin to see improvements in your overall well-being and confidence levels.

Mindfulness and meditation practices offer amazing benefits for loners and individuals experiencing loneliness, serving as invaluable tools for nurturing self-esteem and confidence from within. By integrating these practices into daily life, individuals can embark on a new journey towards creating a more positive mindset and deeper self-assurance.

Mindfulness and meditation empower individuals to develop a deeper understanding and acceptance of themselves. Through regular practice, individuals can explore the inner landscape of their thoughts and emotions, gaining insight into the underlying patterns and beliefs that shape their self-perception. This self-awareness enables individuals to challenge self-limiting beliefs and cultivate a greater sense of self-worth and strength. Incorporating mindfulness and meditation into one's daily routine is a powerful act of self-care and self-empowerment.

Remember, you are not alone in your journey to building confidence, with the help of mindfulness and meditation, you can create a strong foundation of self-esteem that will carry you through any challenges you may face.

Healthy Habits for Physical and Mental Well-being

To thrive as a loner and build self-esteem, it is important to prioritize healthy habits for both physical and mental well-being. Taking care of your body and mind can have a significant impact on how you feel about yourself and your overall confidence levels. By incorporating these habits into your daily routine, you can improve your quality of life and boost your self-esteem.

Engaging in activities that foster personal growth and fulfillment can contribute to a sense of purpose and confidence. Whether it's pursuing hobbies, learning new skills, or volunteering in the community, investing time and energy in activities that resonate with your passions and values can enhance self-esteem and enrich your life.

One key healthy habit for physical well-being is regular exercise. Physical activity not only helps to keep your body in shape, but it also releases endorphins that can improve your mood and reduce feelings of loneliness. Whether it's going for a walk, practicing yoga, or hitting the gym, finding an exercise routine that works for you can have a positive impact on your mental health and self-esteem.

Another important aspect of physical well-being is nutrition. Eating a balanced diet that includes plenty of fruits, vegetables, whole grains, and lean proteins can provide your body with the nutrients it needs to function at its best. Avoiding processed foods and sugary snacks can also help to improve your energy levels and overall health, which can in turn boost your confidence and self-esteem.

In addition to physical health, it is crucial to prioritize your mental well-being as a loner. This can include practices such as mindfulness meditation, journaling, or therapy to help you process your emotions and thoughts. Taking care of your mental health can help you to feel more grounded, centered, and confident in yourself and your abilities.

Building a strong support system of friends, family, or a life coach can also contribute to your overall well-being as a loner. Having a trusted confidant to talk to can provide you with emotional support, guidance, and encouragement to help you work through feelings of loneliness and build your self-esteem. By incorporating these healthy habits into your life, you can take steps towards improving your physical and mental well-being and building confidence from within as a loner.

——

It's important to approach self-esteem building as an ongoing journey rather than a destination. Embrace self-compassion and celebrate small victories along the way. Remember that building self-esteem takes time and effort, but by prioritizing healthy habits, nurturing meaningful connections, and practicing self-acceptance, you can cultivate a deep sense of confidence and well-being that reaches far beyond the challenges of loneliness.

A Guide to Building Self-esteem for Loners

Chapter 6: Overcoming Social Anxiety

Understanding Social Anxiety

Social anxiety is a common issue that many loners and people feeling alone struggle with on a daily basis. It is a condition characterized by an intense fear of social situations and interactions, which can often lead to feelings of self-doubt, isolation, and low self-esteem. In order to overcome social anxiety, it is important to first understand what it is and how it affects your life.

One aspect of social anxiety is the fear of being judged or rejected by others. This fear can be crippling and can make it difficult for individuals to engage in social activities or form meaningful relationships. It is important to recognize that these fears are often irrational and do not accurately reflect how others perceive you. By challenging these negative beliefs and learning to reframe your thoughts, you can begin to build the confidence needed to overcome social anxiety.

Another aspect of social anxiety is the physical symptoms that often go with it, such as sweating, trembling, and rapid heartbeat. These symptoms can be distressing and can make it even more difficult to engage in social situations. By learning relaxation techniques, such as deep breathing and mindfulness, you can begin to manage these physical symptoms and feel more at ease in social settings.

It's crucial to acknowledge that social anxiety is the number one challenge faced by numerous individuals, and experiencing such feelings is not uncommon. Many people grapple with the fear of judgment or rejection in social situations, and it's essential to recognize that you are not alone in these emotions. By acknowledging and accepting your feelings of social anxiety, you can take proactive steps towards overcoming them and nurturing your self-esteem.

Understanding social anxiety is an important step in overcoming this common issue that many loners and people feeling alone face. By challenging negative beliefs, managing physical symptoms, and seeking support from coaching professionals, you can begin to build the confidence needed to thrive in social situations and form meaningful relationships. You are not alone in your struggles, and with the right tools and support, you can overcome social anxiety and build a strong sense of self-esteem from within.

Overcoming social anxiety is a gradual process that requires patience, persistence, and self-compassion.

Techniques for Managing Social Anxiety

Social anxiety can be a debilitating condition for many loners and individuals who often feel alone in social settings. However, there are various techniques that can be employed to effectively manage and overcome social anxiety. One such technique is the practice of mindfulness, which involves being present in the moment and focusing on one's thoughts and feelings without judgment. By practicing mindfulness, individuals can learn to better control their anxious thoughts and reactions in social situations.

Another helpful technique for managing social anxiety is cognitive-behavioral therapy (CBT). CBT helps individuals find and challenge negative thought patterns and beliefs that contribute to their anxiety. Through CBT, individuals can learn to reframe their thoughts in a more positive and realistic light, reducing their anxiety levels in social settings. This technique can be particularly effective when combined with exposure therapy, which involves gradually exposing oneself to feared social situations in a controlled and supportive environment.

In addition to mindfulness and CBT, relaxation techniques such as deep breathing exercises and progressive muscle relaxation can also be helpful in managing social anxiety. These techniques can help individuals calm their minds and bodies, reducing the physical symptoms of anxiety such as rapid heartbeat and sweating. By incorporating these relaxation techniques into their daily routine, individuals can better prepare themselves for social interactions and feel more confident in handling their anxiety.

Building a strong support system of friends, family, or a therapist can also be instrumental in managing social anxiety. Having a trusted person to talk to about fears and anxieties can provide much-needed reassurance and perspective. Additionally, seeking professional help from a life coach, health and wellness coach, or confidence-building coach can offer valuable guidance and support in overcoming social anxiety and building self-esteem.

Managing social anxiety is a challenging but achievable goal for loners and individuals feeling alone. By incorporating techniques such as mindfulness, CBT, relaxation exercises, and building a support system, individuals can learn to better cope with their anxiety and improve their confidence in social situations. With persistence and self-care, individuals can overcome their social anxiety and build a healthier sense of self-esteem.

Gradual Exposure to Social Situations

Gradual exposure to social situations is indeed a vital part in the journey of building self-confidence, especially for loners and individuals experiencing loneliness. The prospect of socializing with others may evoke feelings of anxiety or apprehension, but it's crucial to recognize that confidence is a skill that can be cultivated through deliberate practice and exposure.

One effective way to gradually expose yourself to social situations is to start small. This could mean simply striking up a conversation with a cashier at a store or asking a coworker about their weekend plans. These small interactions may seem insignificant, but they can help to build your confidence and comfort level in social settings.

As you become more comfortable with these small interactions, you can start to challenge yourself by attending social events or gatherings. This could be as simple as going to a networking event or joining a club or group that aligns with your interests. By gradually exposing yourself to these situations, you will begin to feel more at ease and confident in social settings.

It is important to remember that building self-confidence is a process that takes time and patience. It is okay to feel nervous or anxious when stepping out of your comfort zone, but it is important to push through these feelings and continue to challenge yourself. With each social interaction, you will become more adept at handling social situations and building your confidence.

Gradual exposure to social situations is a key part in building self-esteem for loners and those feeling alone. By starting small and gradually challenging yourself, you can begin to feel more confident and comfortable in social settings. Remember, confidence is a skill that can be developed with practice and perseverance.

———

Building self-confidence is a journey, and it's okay to take it one step at a time. By gradually exposing yourself to social situations, seeking out supportive environments, reframing your mindset, and practicing self-compassion, you can build the confidence needed to work through social interactions with greater ease and authenticity.

A Guide to Building Self-esteem for Loners

Chapter 7: Embracing Your Authentic Self

Discovering Your True Identity

On the road to self-discovery, one of the most important steps is uncovering your true identity. For loners and people feeling alone, this can be a very challenging task. Without the distractions of constant social interactions, it can be easy to lose sight of who you truly are. However, by taking the time to delve deep within yourself, you can begin to uncover the unique qualities and characteristics that make you who you are.

One of the first steps in discovering your true identity is to spend time alone in reflection. This may involve journaling, meditation, or simply taking a long walk in nature. By quieting the noise of the outside world, you can begin to listen to your inner voice and understand what truly brings you joy and fulfillment. This process may take time, but by being patient and compassionate with yourself, you can begin to uncover the essence of who you are at your core.

Another important aspect of discovering your true identity is to explore your passions and interests. What activities bring you a sense of purpose and excitement? What topics or hobbies do you find yourself drawn to time and time again? By engaging in activities that light you up, you can begin to understand what truly makes you unique and special. Whether it's painting, writing, hiking, or cooking, embracing your passions can help you connect with your true self on a deeper level.

Exploring your beliefs and values is a pivotal step in the journey of self-discovery and achieving authenticity. Take the time to reflect on what truly matters to you and what principles shape your worldview. Consider the experiences, relationships, and moments that have shaped your values over time. By gaining clarity on your core values, you can set up a guiding framework for your life and begin to live in alignment with your true self.

A Guide to Building Self-esteem for Loners

Discovering your true identity is a lifelong journey that requires self-reflection, introspection, and a willingness to accept change. By taking the time to explore your passions, values, and beliefs, you can begin to build a strong foundation of self-awareness and self-acceptance. It's important to be guided through this process with compassion and support. By uncovering your true identity, you can empower yourself to live authentically and confidently, knowing that you are worthy and deserving of love and acceptance just as you are.

Uncovering your true identity is a deeply personal process. By aligning your life with your core values, working on self-exploration, and staying open to growth, you can cultivate a more authentic and fulfilling existence. Trust in your journey of self-discovery and celebrate the unique qualities that make you who you are.

Embracing Your Uniqueness

So, let's explore the importance of accepting and celebrating your individuality. As loners, it's common to feel like we don't fit in or that we're somehow different from others. But the truth is, our uniqueness is what sets us apart and makes us special.

One of the first steps to embracing your uniqueness is to truly understand and appreciate what makes you different. Take time to reflect on your strengths, interests, and quirks. These are the things that make you who you are, and they are what make you unique. By acknowledging and accepting these aspects of yourself, you can begin to build confidence in your own identity.

It's essential to recognize that embracing your uniqueness involves more than just accepting yourself, it's about celebrating the qualities that set you apart and staying true to your authentic self, even if it means turning from societal norms or expectations. Society often imposes rigid standards and norms that can pressure individuals to conform, but true fulfillment comes from honoring your individuality and following your own path.

Embracing your uniqueness fosters a sense of empowerment and liberation, allowing you to express yourself authentically and confidently. Rather than seeking validation or approval from others, focus on nurturing a deep sense of self-acceptance and self-love. This involves embracing both your strengths and vulnerabilities, recognizing that they contribute to the richness of your character and experiences.

As loners, it's easy to feel isolated or alone in our uniqueness. But by connecting with others who appreciate and celebrate our differences, we can find a sense of belonging and community. Seek out like-minded individuals who support and uplift you and surround yourself with people who encourage you to be your true self.

Don't underestimate the power of your unique perspective and voice in shaping the world around you. By embracing your individuality and standing firm in your values and beliefs, you have the potential to inspire others, challenge societal norms, and effect meaningful change. Your authenticity is a beacon of light that illuminates the path for others to accept their own uniqueness and live more authentically.

Accepting your uniqueness is a powerful tool for building self-esteem and confidence. By accepting and celebrating what sets you apart from others, you can unlock your full potential and live a more fulfilling and authentic life. Remember, you are special just the way you are, so hold on tightly to your uniqueness and let your light shine brightly.

———

Taking hold of your uniqueness is a courageous act of self-expression and self-affirmation. It's about honoring your truth, showing your quirks and idiosyncrasies, and living authentically in a world that often encourages conformity. By staying true to yourself and embracing your individuality, you not only unlock your full potential but also inspire others to do the same.

Living Authentically and Unapologetically

Living authentically and unapologetically is essential for loners and those who feel alone to truly envelop their uniqueness and build self-esteem. It is about being true to yourself, your values, and your beliefs without seeking validation or approval from others. When you live authentically, you are living in alignment with your true self, which can lead to a greater sense of fulfillment and confidence.

To live authentically means to honor your own needs and desires, even if they may differ from those around you. It is about being unafraid to express your true thoughts and feelings, even if they are unpopular or unconventional. By embracing your authenticity, you are showing the world who you truly are and allowing yourself to be seen and heard for all of your unique qualities.

Living unapologetically means owning your choices and taking responsibility for your actions without feeling the need to justify yourself to others. It is about standing firm in your beliefs and values, even in the face of criticism or judgment.

Living unapologetically is a powerful assertion of self-worth and authenticity. It involves boldly asserting your presence and refusing to compromise your values or beliefs to conform to external expectations. By embracing your true self without reservation or apology, you send a clear message to the world that your worth is non-negotiable and that you refuse to diminish yourself for the comfort or approval of others.

Living unapologetically empowers you to set boundaries and prioritize your own well-being and happiness. It allows you to assertively communicate your needs and desires without fear of judgment or rejection. By honoring your truth and asserting your worth, you cultivate a deep sense of self-respect and self-empowerment that permeates every aspect of your life.

For loners and those feeling alone, living authentically and unapologetically can be a powerful tool for building self-esteem. By embracing who you are and standing confidently in your truth, you are sending a message to yourself and others that you are worthy of respect and acceptance just as you are. This can help you cultivate a sense of inner strength and peace that can carry you through life's challenges.

In the journey towards building self-esteem, living authentically and unapologetically can be life changing. By accepting your uniqueness and owning your truth, you are empowering yourself to live a life that is true to who you are. Remember, you are worthy of love and acceptance just as you are, and by living authentically and unapologetically, you can cultivate a deep sense of self-worth and confidence that will carry you through any situation.

— —

Living unapologetically is a radical act of self-love and self-acceptance. It's about embracing your flaws, quirks, and imperfections and celebrating them as integral parts of your identity. By living unapologetically, you reclaim your power, honor your truth, and pave the way for a life of boundless freedom, joy, and fulfillment.

A Guide to Building Self-esteem for Loners

Chapter 8: Seeking Professional Help

When to Consider Therapy or Counseling

Loneliness can take a toll on our mental and emotional well-being, often leading to feelings of isolation, low self-esteem, and a lack of confidence. If you find yourself struggling with these issues, it may be time to consider therapy or counseling. Therapy can provide a safe and non-judgmental space to explore your feelings and work through your challenges with the help of a trained professional.

One important factor to consider is whether your feelings of loneliness are persistent and affecting your daily life. If you find that your loneliness is becoming overwhelming and interfering with your ability to function at work, in relationships, or in social situations, therapy may be a helpful resource. A therapist can help you find the root causes of your loneliness and develop coping strategies to manage your emotions more effectively.

Another sign that therapy or counseling may be beneficial is if you are experiencing symptoms of depression or anxiety as a result of your loneliness. These mental health conditions can worsen feelings of isolation and make it even more difficult to connect with others. A therapist can provide you with tools and techniques to manage your symptoms and improve your overall well-being.

If you have tried other strategies to combat your loneliness, such as joining clubs or socializing more, but still find yourself feeling isolated, therapy can offer added support. A therapist can help you explore deeper issues that may be contributing to your loneliness, such as past traumas or negative beliefs about yourself. By addressing these underlying issues, you can begin to build a stronger sense of self-esteem and confidence.

Therapy or counseling can be a valuable resource for loners and individuals feeling alone who are looking to improve their mental and emotional well-being. By seeking help from a trained professional, you can gain insight into your feelings of loneliness, develop coping strategies, and work towards building a more fulfilling and connected life. Remember, you are not alone in your struggles, and reaching out for support is a courageous step towards healing and growth.

Finding the Right Therapist

In building self-esteem and confidence, finding the right therapist can be a crucial step. For loners and people feeling alone, seeking professional help can provide the necessary support and guidance to work through their struggles. However, with numerous therapists and counselors available, it can be overwhelming to choose the right one. Here are some tips to help you find the therapist that best suits your needs.

First and foremost, it's important to determine what you're looking for in a therapist. Consider your specific needs and goals for therapy. Are you seeking help with building self-esteem, managing loneliness, or overcoming past traumas? Knowing what you want to work on can help you narrow down your search for a therapist who specializes in those areas.

Once you have a clear idea of what you're looking for, it's time to start researching potential therapists. You can ask for recommendations from friends, family, or trusted professionals in the field. Additionally, websites like Psychology Today and TherapyDen offer directories of therapists where you can filter by specialties, insurance accepted, and location.

When reaching out to potential therapists, don't be afraid to ask questions. Inquire about their approach to therapy, experience working with loners or people feeling alone, and their availability for appointments. It's important to find a therapist who you feel comfortable with and who you believe can help you achieve your goals.

After narrowing down your options, consider scheduling consultations with a few therapists. This will give you the opportunity to meet them in person or virtually and see if you feel a connection. Trust your instincts and choose the therapist who you feel understands your needs and can support you on your journey towards building self-esteem and confidence.

Finding the right therapist is a personal decision and may take time. Don't be discouraged if you don't find the perfect fit on your first try. Keep exploring your options until you find a therapist who you feel comfortable with and who can help you on your path to self-discovery and personal growth.

Support Groups and Resources for Loners

Loners often struggle with feelings of isolation and loneliness, but it's important to know that you are not alone in feeling this way. There are support groups and resources available to help you work through these emotions and build your self-esteem. By connecting with others who understand your struggles, you can find comfort and encouragement in knowing that you are not the only one facing these challenges.

One valuable resource for loners is support groups specifically designed for individuals who struggle with feelings of isolation. These groups provide a safe space for you to share your experiences, connect with others who understand your struggles, and receive support and encouragement from people who are going through similar challenges. Being part of a support group can help you feel less alone and more understood and can provide you with valuable insights and coping strategies for managing your feelings of loneliness.

In addition to support groups, there are also online resources available for loners looking to build their self-esteem and overcome feelings of isolation. Websites, forums, and social media groups dedicated to loners can provide you with a sense of community and connection, even if you prefer to interact with others from the comfort of your own home. These online resources can be a valuable source of support, information, and inspiration for loners looking to improve their self-esteem and build stronger connections with others.

Life coaching, health and wellness coaching, and confidence building coaching are also valuable resources for loners looking to improve their self-esteem and overcome feelings of loneliness. Working with a coach can help you identify and address the underlying issues contributing to your feelings of isolation and can provide you with personalized strategies and techniques for building your confidence and self-worth. A coach can also help you set goals and create a plan for achieving them, so you can start to feel more empowered and in control of your life.

Loners have access to a wide range of support groups and resources to help them build their self-esteem and overcome feelings of isolation. By connecting with others who understand your struggles, seeking out online resources, and working with a coach, you can start to feel more connected, confident, and empowered in your own skin. Remember, you are not alone in feeling lonely, and there are people and resources available to support you on your journey to greater self- esteem and well-being.

A Guide to Building Self-esteem for Loners

Chapter 9: Celebrating Your Progress

Recognizing Your Achievements

In the journey of building self-esteem and confidence, it is important for loners and those feeling alone to take the time to recognize and celebrate their achievements. Often, we are quick to downplay our successes or brush them off as insignificant. However, acknowledging and celebrating our accomplishments is essential for boosting our self-esteem and confidence.

Keeping a journal or list of accomplishments is a valuable practice for recognizing and celebrating your achievements. It's important to note that the definition of achievement extends beyond traditional milestones or praises. It encompasses a wide range of experiences, both big and small, that contribute to your growth and well-being.

Reflecting on your achievements can offer valuable insights into your strengths, values, and passions. Notice recurring themes or patterns in your accomplishments, as they may offer clues about areas where you excel or experiences that bring you joy. This self-awareness can inform your future goals and aspirations, guiding you towards paths that align with your authentic self.

Another way to recognize your achievements is to share them with others. Loners and those feeling alone may be hesitant to seek validation from others, but sharing your successes with a trusted friend, family member, or coach can be incredibly validating. It can also help you see your achievements through someone else's eyes, giving you a fresh perspective on your accomplishments.

It is also important to set aside time to celebrate your achievements, whether it's treating yourself to a special meal, buying yourself a small gift, or simply taking a moment to bask in your success. By celebrating your achievements, you are reinforcing your self-worth and sending a message to yourself that you are deserving of recognition and praise.

Recognizing your achievements is a crucial step in building self-esteem and confidence. By acknowledging your successes, sharing them with others, and celebrating them in meaningful ways, you are affirming your worth and boosting your self-confidence. Remember, you are worthy of recognition and praise, and your achievements deserve to be celebrated.

——

Recognizing your achievements is a powerful practice that fuels self-esteem and personal growth. By embracing a holistic view of accomplishment and celebrating your progress along the way, you honor your journey and affirm your inherent worthiness.

Setting New Goals and Challenges

Setting new goals and challenges is an important part of building self-esteem and confidence for loners and individuals who may be feeling alone. By establishing new goals and challenges, you are pushing yourself out of your comfort zone and embracing personal growth. It is important to remember that setting goals doesn't have to be daunting or overwhelming. Start small and gradually work your way up to more challenging goals.

One way to set new goals and challenges is to reflect on your current situation and find areas of your life where you would like to see improvement. This could be in your career, relationships, health, or personal development. Once you have found these areas, set specific and achievable goals that will help you progress towards a more fulfilling life. Remember to be realistic with your goals and break them down into smaller, manageable steps.

Challenges serve as invaluable opportunities for personal growth and self-discovery. They push you to expand your horizons, test your abilities, and uncover hidden strengths and power. While stepping outside of your comfort zone may feel daunting, it's important to recognize that embracing challenges is a journey that leads to profound self-growth and empowerment.

Challenges provide a platform for learning and skill development. As you travel through unfamiliar territory and confront obstacles, you get new knowledge, insights, and competencies that broaden your perspective and enhance your capabilities. Accept each challenge as an opportunity for growth and self-improvement, recognizing that every setback is a steppingstone towards mastery and personal evolution.

It is important to encourage yourself and to set new goals and challenges. By identifying areas for improvement and supporting in your journey towards personal growth, you are helping yourself take control of your life and build the confidence you need to succeed. Encourage yourself to step outside of your comfort zone and take on new experiences that will help you grow and thrive.

Setting new goals and challenges is a powerful tool for building self-esteem and confidence for loners and individuals feeling alone. By pushing yourself out of your comfort zone, you are embracing personal growth and proving to yourself that you are capable of achieving great things. Remember to start small, be realistic with your goals, and seek support from a coach or mentor if needed. Grab on to challenges as opportunities for growth and self-discovery and watch as your confidence and self-esteem soar to new heights.

Challenges are not merely obstacles to overcome but opportunities for transformation and empowerment. Utilize the unknown with courage and strength, knowing that each challenge you conquer brings you one step closer to realizing your full potential and living a life of purpose and fulfillment.

Building a Support System for Continued Growth

As loners, it can be easy to fall into the trap of isolating ourselves and believing that we can handle everything on our own. However, building a strong support system is crucial for our continued growth and well-being. By surrounding ourselves with positive and supportive individuals, we can gain new perspectives, receive encouragement, and build lasting connections that can help us face life's challenges.

One of the first steps in building a support system is to identify the people in our lives who lift us up and make us feel valued. These may be friends, family members, or even acquaintances who share similar interests and values. It's important to cultivate these relationships and make an effort to stay connected, whether through regular meetups, phone calls, or text messages. By nurturing these connections, we can create a sense of belonging and security that can bolster our self-esteem and confidence.

In addition to personal relationships, seeking out professional support can also be beneficial for loners looking to build a support system. Life coaches, health and wellness coaches, and confidence building coaches can provide valuable guidance and tools to help us overcome obstacles, set goals, and achieve personal growth. These professionals offer a non-judgmental space for us to explore our thoughts and feelings and can help us develop a plan for moving forward in a positive direction.

Another important aspect of building a support system is learning to ask for help when we need it. As loners, we may be accustomed to handling things on our own, but there is strength in vulnerability and reaching out for support. Whether we're struggling with self-doubt, stress, or loneliness, opening up to trusted individuals can help us feel heard and understood, and can lead to valuable insights and solutions that we may not have considered on our own.

Building a support system is an ongoing journey that involves deliberate effort and commitment. While loners may value their independence and solitude, building meaningful connections and seeking support from others is essential for overall well-being and personal growth.

Practicing vulnerability is a key part of building authentic connections and building trust within your support system. It involves being open and honest about your thoughts, feelings, and experiences, even if it feels uncomfortable or challenging. By allowing yourself to be vulnerable with trusted individuals, you create opportunities for deeper connection, strengthening the bonds of your relationships.

Building a support system is a dynamic and evolving process that requires nurturing and investment. By prioritizing relationships, seeking professional guidance, practicing vulnerability, and embracing reciprocity, loners can cultivate a robust network of support that helps build personal growth, and confidence. Remember that you are not meant to face life's challenges alone, and by surrounding yourself with positive influences and seeking help when needed, you can create a community that propels you towards a brighter, more fulfilling future.

A Guide to Building Self-esteem for Loners

Chapter 10: Moving Forward with Confidence

Reflecting on Your Journey

As loners, it can be easy to get caught up in feelings of isolation and self-doubt. However, taking the time to reflect on your journey can be a powerful tool for building self-esteem and confidence. Reflecting on where you have been, where you are now, and where you want to go can help you gain perspective and see how much you have grown.

When reflecting on your journey, it's important to focus on both the challenges and successes you have faced. Acknowledge the obstacles you have overcome and the progress you have made, no matter how small it may seem. Celebrate your victories, no matter how insignificant they may seem to others. By recognizing your achievements, you can boost your self- esteem and remind yourself of your worth.

Take the time to identify the patterns and habits that have helped or hindered your progress. Are there certain behaviors or thought patterns that have held you back? Are there habits that have helped you move forward? By reflecting on these aspects of your journey, you can make conscious choices to change what isn't working and reinforce what is.

Reflecting on your journey is not only about acknowledging past achievements but also about gaining clarity and direction for the future. In addition to setting short-term goals for the coming days, weeks, or months, consider envisioning your long-term goals and dreams. What do you hope to accomplish in the next year, five years, or even ten years? By taking the time to visualize your ideal future and identify your core values and priorities, you can create a roadmap for personal and professional growth that aligns with your authentic self. Remember, it's okay to start small and take things one step at a time. Progress is progress, no matter how slow.

Setting specific, measurable, achievable, relevant, and time-bound (SMART) goals can help you turn your aspirations into actionable steps. Break down your goals into smaller milestones and create a detailed plan outlining the tasks and deadlines needed to achieve them. This approach not only provides a clear roadmap for success but also instills a sense of accountability and motivation to stay on track.

Goal setting is a powerful tool for building confidence. By visualizing your goals, creating a plan to achieve them, and still being flexible and adaptable along the way, you can cultivate a sense of purpose and direction that propels you towards a future filled with fulfillment and success.

Reflecting on your journey is a powerful tool for building self-esteem and confidence. By acknowledging your successes, identifying your obstacles, and setting goals for the future, you can gain a deeper understanding of yourself and your abilities.

Remember, you are not alone in your journey. Reach out for support and guidance along the way. Take on your journey and trust in your ability to grow and thrive.

Strategies for Maintaining Confidence

In the journey of building self-esteem and confidence, loners and individuals experiencing loneliness can benefit greatly from developing a repertoire of strategies designed to cultivate and sustain their sense of self-assurance. These strategies serve as essential tools for navigating the challenges of isolation and self-doubt, encouraging individuals to accept their uniqueness and lead more fulfilling lives. Here are several key strategies that loners can incorporate into their daily lives to maintain confidence:

Positive Self-Talk: Practice creating a compassionate and supportive inner dialogue. Challenge negative self-beliefs and replace them with affirming statements that reinforce your worth and capabilities. Remind yourself of past accomplishments and strengths whenever self-doubt creeps in.

Loners often struggle with feelings of self-doubt and worthlessness, which can erode their confidence over time. By consciously reframing negative thoughts and beliefs about oneself, individuals can cultivate a more positive and stronger mindset. Affirmations such as "I am worthy of love and respect" or "I am capable of achieving my goals" can help loners build confidence and self-esteem.

Set Achievable Goals: Break down larger aspirations into smaller, manageable tasks and set realistic goals for yourself. Celebrate each milestone achieved along the way, no matter how small, as it contributes to your overall progress and confidence.

Setting realistic goals and taking small steps towards achieving them can be a powerful strategy for keeping confidence. Loners may feel overwhelmed by the prospect of making significant changes in their lives, but by breaking down their goals into manageable tasks, they can build momentum and confidence over time. Celebrating small victories along the way can also boost self-esteem and motivation.

Seek Personal Growth Opportunities: Accept opportunities for learning and self-improvement that align with your interests and passions. Whether it's pursuing further education, developing new skills, or exploring creative outlets, investing in your personal growth fosters a sense of competence and self-assurance.

Establish Boundaries: Set clear boundaries in your relationships and daily interactions to protect your well-being and preserve your sense of autonomy. Learn to say no to requests or obligations that do not align with your values or priorities and prioritize activities that nourish your mental and emotional health.

Practice Self-Care: Prioritize self-care practices that nurture your physical, mental, and emotional well-being. Engage in activities that bring you joy and relaxation, such as meditation, exercise, spending time in nature, or indulging in hobbies that replenish your spirit.

This includes taking care of your physical, emotional, and mental well-being. Loners can benefit from engaging in activities that bring them joy and relaxation, such as reading a book, going for a walk in nature, or practicing mindfulness and meditation. By prioritizing self-care, individuals can boost their self-esteem and confidence levels.

Connect with Supportive Individuals: Cultivate meaningful connections with individuals who appreciate and celebrate your unique qualities. Surround yourself with people who uplift and support you and seek out social interactions that leave you feeling valued and understood.

Seeking support from others is another crucial strategy for keeping confidence as a loner. While it may be tempting to isolate oneself when feeling alone, reaching out to friends, family, or a support group can provide valuable encouragement and perspective. Connecting with others who share similar experiences can also help loners feel less isolated and more validated in their struggles.

Celebrate Your Achievements: Take time to acknowledge and celebrate your accomplishments, no matter how small. Recognize your progress and growth and allow yourself to bask in the satisfaction of your efforts. Celebrating your successes reinforces your belief in your abilities and bolsters your confidence for future endeavors.

———

Practicing self-compassion and forgiveness is essential for maintaining confidence as a loner. It is important to recognize that everyone makes mistakes and faces challenges in life, and that it is okay to be imperfect. By treating oneself with kindness and understanding, individuals can cultivate a sense of worthiness and self-acceptance that is essential for building confidence from within.

Embracing a Life filled with Self-Esteem and Connection

Let's explore the importance of embracing a life filled with self-esteem and connection, particularly for those who may be experiencing feelings of loneliness or isolation. Loners, or individuals who often find themselves feeling alone, can benefit greatly from creating a sense of self-worth and forming meaningful connections with others. By creating a strong sense of self-worth and building meaningful connections with others, individuals can mitigate the negative impacts of loneliness and experience greater fulfillment and happiness.

First and foremost, developing self-esteem is crucial for combating feelings of isolation and inadequacy. Self-esteem serves as a foundation for good self-confidence, enabling individuals to face life's challenges with greater ease and positivity. By recognizing their inherent worth and embracing their unique qualities, loners can cultivate a deep sense of self-assurance that empowers them to engage with the world more confidently and authentically.

Embracing a life filled with self-esteem and connection can lead to greater overall satisfaction and happiness. Research consistently shows that individuals with strong social support networks and healthy self-esteem tend to experience better mental and emotional well-being. By prioritizing self-care, nurturing meaningful relationships, and building a positive self-image, loners can create a life rich in fulfillment, joy, and meaningful connections.

One of the first steps in building self-esteem is to recognize and appreciate your own worth. It's important to understand that you are valuable and deserving of love and respect, regardless of how others may perceive you. By embracing a positive self-image, you can begin to cultivate a sense of confidence that will help you be comfortable in social interactions and build deeper connections with others.

Another key aspect of building self-esteem is to practice self-care and self-compassion. This means taking the time to prioritize your own well-being, both physically and emotionally. By engaging in activities that bring you joy and fulfillment, such as exercise, meditation, or creative pursuits, you can boost your self-esteem and build a stronger sense of self.

Connecting with others is also crucial for loners looking to build self-esteem and combat feelings of loneliness. Building relationships with like-minded individuals who share your values and interests can provide a sense of belonging and support that is essential for mental and emotional well-being. By reaching out to others and fostering meaningful connections, you can create a sense of community and belonging that will help you thrive.

By embracing a life filled with self-esteem and connection, loners can transform feelings of loneliness and isolation into opportunities for growth and self-discovery. Through practicing self-care, building confidence, and forming meaningful connections with others, you can create a life that is rich in fulfillment and purpose. Remember, you are worthy of love and belonging, and by embracing these principles, you can cultivate a sense of confidence from within that will empower you to live a life that is truly fulfilling.

A Guide to Building Self-esteem for Loners

Identifying Strengths and Weaknesses

1. What tasks or activities do you excel at and enjoy doing?
2. In what areas do others often seek your advice or help?
3. What accomplishments are you most proud of in your life?
4. What skills or talents do you believe set you apart from others?
5. What feedback have you received from others about your strengths?
6. What tasks or situations make you feel energized and motivated?
7. What challenges or obstacles have you successfully overcome in the past?
8. Are there any patterns or themes in your past successes and failures?
9. What do you believe are your top three strengths and why?
10. In what areas do you feel you could improve or develop further?
11. What tasks or skills do you tend to avoid or struggle with?
12. How do you react to criticism or feedback about your performance?
13. Are there any recurring obstacles or challenges you face in your life?
14. How do you handle stressful or high-pressure situations?
15. What values are most important to you in your personal and professional life?
16. How do you approach learning and getting new skills or knowledge?
17. What do you believe are your biggest opportunities for growth and development?
18. How do you prioritize and manage your time effectively?
19. What do you enjoy learning about or exploring in your free

time?

20. How do you see yourself contributing to the world or making a positive impact?

Setting Realistic Goals

1. What specific outcome do you want to achieve with this goal?
2. Is this goal aligned with your values, passions, and long-term aspirations?
3. What steps or actions are necessary to reach this goal?
4. Have you broken down the goal into smaller, manageable tasks or milestones?
5. What resources or support do you need to carry out this goal?
6. How will you measure progress and track your success along the way?
7. Have you set a realistic timeline for achieving this goal?
8. What potential obstacles or challenges might you encounter, and how will you overcome them?
9. Are you willing to adjust your approach or timeline if needed to stay on track?
10. How will achieving this goal positively change your life or the lives of others?

Ways to engage in self-care

1. Practice mindfulness: Spend time in quiet reflection, focusing on the present moment.

2. Read a book: Escape into a good book that interests and inspires you.

3. Take a nature walk: Enjoy the outdoors and connect with the beauty of nature.

4. Journal: Write down your thoughts, feelings, and reflections to gain clarity and insight.

5. Meditate: Clear your mind and relax through meditation or deep breathing exercises.

6. Indulge in a hobby: Engage in activities you love, whether it's painting, cooking, or playing music.

7. Pamper yourself: Treat yourself to a spa day at home with a bubble bath, face mask, or self-massage.

8. Practice yoga: Stretch your body, improve flexibility, and promote relaxation through yoga practice.

9. Listen to music: Create a playlist of your favorite songs to uplift your mood and soothe your soul.

10. Cook a healthy meal: Nourish your body with nutritious and delicious homemade food.

11. Watch a movie: Enjoy a movie night with your favorite films or documentaries.

12. Declutter your space: Organize and tidy up your living environment to create a sense of calm and order.

13. Get creative: Express yourself through art, writing, or crafting to unleash your creativity.

14. Connect with a pet: Spend time with a furry friend for companionship and comfort.

15. Practice self-compassion: Be kind to yourself, acknowledge your worth, and treat yourself with love and understanding.

Mindfulness Meditations

1. Breath Awareness: Find a quiet space, sit comfortably, and focus on your breath. Inhale deeply, exhale slowly, and observe the sensations of each breath without judgment.
2. Body Scan: Lie down or sit comfortably, close your eyes, and bring awareness to each part of your body, starting from your toes up to your head. Notice any tension or sensations without trying to change them.
3. Loving-Kindness: Sit quietly and send loving-kindness to yourself, repeating phrases like "May I be happy, may I be healthy, may I be at peace." Then extend these wishes to others in your life.
4. Nature Visualization: Imagine yourself in a peaceful natural setting, such as a forest or by the ocean. Visualize the sights, sounds, and sensations of being in that serene environment.
5. Gratitude Meditation: Reflect on three things you are grateful for in your life. Focus on the feelings of gratitude and appreciation for these blessings.
6. Mantra Meditation: Choose a calming word or phrase, such as "peace" or "I am enough," and repeat it silently as you meditate. Let the mantra guide your thoughts and bring you back to the present moment.
7. Silent Walking Meditation: Take a slow, mindful walk in nature or around your home. Pay attention to each step you take, the sensations in your body, and the sounds around you.
8. Candle Gazing: Light a candle in a dark room and focus on the flame. Watch the flickering light and let your mind settle into a state of calm and stillness.
9. Mindful Eating: Choose a small snack or meal and eat it slowly, savoring each bite. Pay attention to the flavors, textures, and sensations of the food as you consume it

mindfully.

10. Stargazing Meditation: Find a quiet spot outdoors at night, lie down, and gaze at the stars above. Allow yourself to feel connected to the vastness of the universe and contemplate your place in it.

Managing Social Anxiety

1. Practice deep breathing: When you feel anxious, take slow, deep breaths to calm your nervous system and reduce physical tension.

2. Challenge negative thoughts: Find and challenge negative beliefs about social situations by questioning their validity and replacing them with more realistic and positive thoughts.

3. Gradual exposure: Gradually expose yourself to social situations that trigger anxiety, starting with small steps and gradually increasing the level of exposure over time.

4. Mindfulness meditation: Practice mindfulness to stay present in the moment, see your thoughts and feelings without judgment, and cultivate a sense of calm and acceptance.

5. Set realistic goals: Set achievable goals for social interactions, such as starting a conversation with one person or attending a small gathering and celebrating your successes no matter how small.

6. Seek support: Talk to a trusted friend, therapist, or support group about your social anxiety to gain perspective, encouragement, and coping strategies.

7. Learn relaxation techniques: Practice relaxation techniques such as progressive muscle relaxation, guided imagery, or yoga to reduce stress and anxiety levels.

8. Focus on the conversation: Shift your focus from your internal worries to actively listening and engaging in the conversation, showing genuine interest in others and their perspectives.

9. Use positive self-talk: Replace self-critical thoughts with positive affirmations and reminders of your strengths and past successes in social situations.

10. Take care of yourself: Prioritize self-care by getting enough rest, eating well, exercising regularly, and engaging in activities that bring you joy and relaxation.

Daily Confirmations
A Guide to Building Self-esteem for Loners

1. Day 1: "I am worthy of love and respect just as I am."

Day 2: "I choose to focus on what I can control and let go of what I cannot." Day 3: "I am capable of overcoming any challenges that come my way."

Day 4: "I deserve to prioritize my well- being and happiness."

Day 5: "I am grateful for the progress I have made on my journey."

Day 6: "I trust in my ability to make the best decisions for myself."

Day 7: "I am enough, just as I am, and I deserve to be kind to myself."

Day 8: "I release all negative thoughts and embrace positivity."

Day 9: "I am resilient and can bounce back from setbacks."

Day 10: "I am proud of how far I have come and excited for where I am going." Day 11: "I choose to see challenges as opportunities for growth."

Day 12: "I am in control of my thoughts and choose to focus on the positive." Day 13: "I am surrounded by love and support, even in moments of solitude." Day 14: "I forgive myself for past mistakes and embrace self-compassion." Day 15: "I am worthy of success and abundance in all areas of my life."

Day 16: "I radiate positivity and attract positive energy into my life."

Day 17: "I am a work in progress, and that is perfectly okay."

Day 18: "I am open to new possibilities and opportunities that come my way."

Day 19: "I trust in my intuition to guide me towards what is best for me."

Day 20: "I am a unique individual with valuable contributions to offer."

Day 21: "I choose to see the beauty in myself and others."

Day 22: "I am resilient, strong, and capable of handling whatever comes my way."

Day 23: "I am deserving of self-care and moments of relaxation."

Day 24: "I release all self-doubt and embrace my inner strength."

Day 25: "I am grateful for the lessons learned from past challenges."

Day 26: "I am confident in my abilities and trust in my potential."

Day 27: "I am surrounded by positivity and love, even in moments of darkness."

Day 28: "I am a beacon of light, spreading positivity wherever I go.

Day 29: "I am worthy of all the good things that life has to offer."

Day 30: "I am proud of the progress I have made and excited for the journey ahead."

A Guide to Building Self-esteem for Loners

Boosting Your Self-confidence
A Guide to Building Self-esteem for Loners

Day 1: Start your day with positive affirmations about your abilities and strengths.

Day 2: Set small, achievable goals for the day and celebrate your accomplishments.

Day 3: Practice self-care activities that make you feel good about yourself.

Day 4: Challenge negative self-talk by replacing it with positive thoughts.

Day 5: Surround yourself with supportive and positive people who uplift you.

Day 6: Step out of your comfort zone and try something new to boost your confidence.

Day 7: Reflect on past successes and remind yourself of your capabilities.

Day 8: Dress in a way that makes you feel confident and empowered.

Day 9: Practice good posture and body language to exude confidence.

Day 10: Engage in activities that align with your passions and strengths.

Day 11: Seek feedback from others to gain perspective on your strengths.

Day 12: Practice mindfulness and focus on the present moment to build inner confidence.

Day 13: Visualize success in challenging situations to boost your confidence.

Day 14: Take time to appreciate your progress and growth on your self-confidence journey.

Day 15: Learn from setbacks and use them as opportunities to strengthen your resilience.

Day 16: Practice gratitude for the qualities and skills that make you unique.

Day 17: Engage in positive self-talk and affirmations throughout the day.

Day 18: Volunteer or help others to boost your sense of self-worth.

Day 19: Set boundaries to protect your self- esteem and well-being.

Day 20: Accept constructive criticism as a tool for growth and improvement.

Day 21: Engage in physical exercise to boost your confidence and mood.

Day 22: Reflect on your values and align your actions with what is important to you.

Day 23: Take on a leadership role or project to showcase your skills and abilities.

Day 24: Practice self-compassion and forgive yourself for any perceived shortcomings.

Day 25: Celebrate your uniqueness and enjoy what sets you apart from others.

Day 26: Surround yourself with positive affirmations and reminders of your worth.

Day 27: Engage in positive visualization exercises to boost your confidence.

Day 28: Reflect on your achievements and the obstacles you have overcome.

Day 29: Share your successes and accomplishments with others to reinforce your confidence.

Connecting with others

Join a club or group that interests you.

Attend networking events or conferences.

Volunteer for a cause or organization you are passionate about.

Attend social gatherings or parties.

Take a class or workshop in something new.

Join a sports team or fitness group.

Attend community events or festivals.

Reach out to old friends or acquaintances to catch up.

Attend a meetup or group activity in your area.

Join a book club or discussion group.

Attend a religious or spiritual service.

Use social media to connect with others with similar interests.

Attend a community service project or clean-up event.

Participate in a charity fundraiser or event.

Take a group exercise class.

Attend a lecture or seminar.

Join a professional organization in your field.

Attend a cultural event or performance.

Participate in a group travel experience or tour.

Use a networking app or website to connect with others in your area.

Strategies for maintaining confidence

1. Practice self-affirmations: Remind yourself of your worth, strengths, and capabilities through positive self-talk and affirmations.

2. Set boundaries: Set up boundaries that protect your time, energy, and well-being, and communicate them assertively to others.

3. Engage in self-care: Prioritize self-care activities that nurture your physical, mental, and emotional health, such as exercise, meditation, or hobbies you enjoy.

4. Celebrate your achievements: Acknowledge and celebrate your accomplishments, no matter how small, to boost your self-esteem and motivation.

5. Enjoy solitude: Your alone time is an opportunity for self-reflection, creativity, and personal growth.

6. Challenge yourself: Set challenging but achievable goals that push you out of your comfort zone and help you build confidence through accomplishment.

7. Surround yourself with positivity: Surround yourself with supportive and uplifting people who encourage and inspire you to be your best self.

8. Practice gratitude: Cultivate a mindset of gratitude by focusing on the positive aspects of your life and expressing appreciation for the blessings you have.

9. Learn from setbacks: View setbacks and failures as learning opportunities that can strengthen your determination to succeed.

10. Stay true to yourself: Honor your values, beliefs, and passions, and stay true to who you are, even when faced with external pressures or expectations.

These strategies can help you maintain confidence, self-assurance, and a positive self-image as you walk your personal growth journey.

Setting New Goals and Challenges

1. **What lessons or insights did you gain from the book that you want to apply to your life?**

2. **How has your perspective on self-validation and self-appreciation shifted after reading the book?**

3. **What areas of your life do you feel inspired to improve or change based on the book's message?**

4. **In what ways can you show more self-compassion and celebrate your own achievements moving forward?**

5. **What new goals do you want to set for yourself to align with the book's themes of self-empowerment and self-recognition?**

6. **How can you challenge yourself to step out of your comfort zone and accept new opportunities for growth?**

7. **Are there any limiting beliefs or self-doubts that you want to overcome in pursuit of your goals?**

8. **What support or resources do you need to help you achieve your new goals and face new challenges?**

9. **How will you measure your progress and celebrate your milestones along the way?**

10. **What daily habits or practices can you implement to reinforce self-appreciation and self-motivation in your life?**

Reflecting on these questions can help you clarify your aspirations, set meaningful goals, and accept new challenges with confidence and self-assurance.

1. Reflection: Today, I acknowledge my worth and celebrate my unique qualities.

Positive Footnote: Remember, you are enough just as you are.

2. Reflection: I believe solitude is an opportunity for self-discovery and growth.

Positive Footnote: Your alone time is a gift for self-reflection and creativity.

3. Reflection: I set boundaries that honor my needs and protect my well-being.

Positive Footnote: Boundaries are a form of self-care and self-respect.

4. Reflection: I practice self-compassion and treat myself with kindness and understanding.

Positive Footnote: Be gentle with yourself, you're doing the best you can.

5. Reflection: I challenge myself to step out of my comfort zone and take on new opportunities.

Positive Footnote: Growth happens outside of your comfort zone.

6. Reflection: I focus on the present moment and let go of worries about the past or future.

Positive Footnote: Today is a gift, that's why it's called the present.

7. Reflection: I express gratitude for the blessings and opportunities in my life.

Positive Footnote: Gratitude opens the door to abundance and joy.

8. Reflection: I practice mindfulness to stay grounded and centered in the midst of chaos.

Positive Footnote: In stillness, you find clarity and peace.

9. Reflection: I seek support and connection with others who uplift and inspire me.

Positive Footnote: Surround yourself with positivity and encouragement.

1. Reflection: I celebrate my progress and achievements, no matter how small they may seem.

Positive Footnote: Every step forward is a victory worth celebrating.

1. Reflection: I accept my strengths and use them to overcome
    challenges with confidence.

Positive Footnote: Your strengths are your superpowers, use
them wisely.

12. Reflection: I learn from setbacks and failures, seeing them as steppingstones to success.

Positive Footnote: Failure is not the opposite of success, it's part of the journey.

1. Reflection: I prioritize self-care and nourish my mind, body, and soul with love and attention.

Positive Footnote: Self-care is not selfish, it's essential for your well-being.

14. Reflection: I practice gratitude for the simple joys and moments of beauty in my day.

Positive Footnote: Find joy in the little things, for they are the big things in life.

15. Reflection: I set new goals that challenge and inspire me to grow beyond my limits.

Positive Footnote: Dream big, work hard, and believe in yourself.

16. Reflection: I release self-doubt and hold on to self-confidence in my abilities and potential.

Positive Footnote: You are capable of achieving great things, believe in yourself.

17. Reflection: I show myself compassion and forgiveness for my mistakes and imperfections.

Positive Footnote: Imperfection is beauty, embrace your uniqueness.

18. Reflection: I practice patience and trust in the timing of my journey towards self-discovery.

Positive Footnote: Trust the process, everything unfolds in divine timing.

19. Reflection: I engage in activities that bring me joy and fulfillment, nurturing my soul.

Positive Footnote: Follow your passions, they lead you to your purpose.

1. Reflection: I listen to my inner voice and intuition, trusting my instincts and inner wisdom.

Positive Footnote: Your intuition is your inner compass, guiding you towards your true north.

1. Reflection: I let go of comparison and accept my
    individuality and uniqueness.

Positive Footnote: Comparison is the thief of joy, celebrate
your uniqueness.

1. Reflection: I practice self-discipline and consistency in pursuing my goals and dreams.

Positive Footnote: Consistency is the key to success, keep moving forward.

23. Reflection: I seek moments of stillness and silence to recharge and rejuvenate my spirit.

Positive Footnote: In silence, you find clarity and inner peace.

24. Reflection: I express my creativity and authenticity in everything I do, honoring my true self.

Positive Footnote: Your authenticity is your power, shine brightly.

25. Reflection: I let go of fear and hold on to courage in facing challenges and uncertainties.

Positive Footnote: Courage is not the absence of fear, but the triumph over it.

26. Reflection: I practice forgiveness towards myself and others, releasing resentment and negativity.

Positive Footnote: Forgiveness is freedom, let go of the past and live in the present.

27. Reflection: I nourish my mind with positive thoughts and beliefs that empower and uplift me.

Positive Footnote: Your thoughts create your reality, choose them wisely.

28. Reflection: I express love and kindness towards myself and others, spreading positivity and light.

Positive Footnote: Love is the highest vibration, share it generously.

29. Reflection: I reflect on my growth and evolution, acknowledging the progress I've made on my journey.

Positive Footnote: You are constantly evolving and growing, celebrate your transformation.

30. Reflection: I clap for myself, recognizing my worth and inner strength.

Positive Footnote: Clap for yourself, you are your own biggest cheerleader and supporter.

These daily reflections and positive footnotes can serve as reminders of your worth, potential, and inner power as you continue your journey of self-discovery and personal growth. Embrace each day with gratitude, self-compassion, and a belief in your ability to overcome challenges and achieve your dreams.

Embracing Solitude, Finding Connection

I sit here, pen in hand, reflecting on my journey, I am reminded of the solitude that has been my constant companion since childhood. My name is Katie Rose, and I have always been a loner. Growing up, I found peace in the quiet corners of my mind, away from the noise and chaos of the world around me. I found that nature was a source of solitude I enjoyed and would sit under a tree, weather permitting, and just listen to the sounds that surrounded me. While my solitude nurtured a fierce independence within me, it also brought with it, bouts of depression and loneliness that I struggled to work through alone.

From a young age, I was different from my friends. While they sought out companionship and thrived in social settings, I found comfort in my own company. I was content to lose myself in books, art, and nature, finding beauty and meaning in the quiet moments of reflection. However, as I grew older, I realized that my isolation was not just a choice but a shield I had built around myself, keeping others at arm's length, including my own family.

The lack of close friends did not bother me at first. I was used to being on my own even in my marriage, finding strength in my solitude and independence. But as life presented its challenges and hardships, I found myself facing moments of deep despair and longing for connection. In those times of need, I had no one to turn to, no shoulder to lean on, and the weight of my loneliness felt suffocating.

My introverted nature only added to the complexity of my struggles. While I cherished my alone time and valued introspection, I found it difficult to reach out to others, to let down my guard and allow them into my world. The fear of rejection, judgment, and vulnerability kept me trapped in a cycle of isolation and self-imposed exile from the world outside.

Life has a way of nudging us out of our comfort zones, of pushing us towards growth and transformation, even when we resist it with all our might. Circumstances beyond my control forced me to confront my fears, to step out of the shadows of my solitude and into the light of possibility. It was a journey filled with uncertainty, self-doubt, and moments of despair, but it was also a journey of determination, and faith in the power of the human spirit to rise above adversity.

Through sheer drive and determination, I began to remake my life, brick by brick, layer by layer. I sought out opportunities for connection, for community, for belonging. I took small steps towards building relationships with like-minded individuals who shared my values, passions, and dreams. I opened myself up to the possibility of friendship, of camaraderie, of love in its many forms.

Slowly but surely, I am creating a tribe of friends who accepted me for who I am, who see beyond the walls I have erected around my life, and who accept me with open arms. These kindred spirits are my pillars of support, my confidants, my chosen family. They stand by me in moments of joy and sorrow, offering a listening ear, a comforting presence, and a sense of belonging that I have longed for all my life.

In parallel, I have embarked on a journey of reconnecting with my family, bridging the gaps that had formed over the years of silence and distance. I am reaching out to my siblings and other relatives and reconnecting through the power of social media.

While I worked through the twists and turns of my path towards self-discovery and personal growth, I felt compelled to share my story, my struggles, my triumphs with the world. The book "When No One is Clapping, You Must Clap for Yourself" was born out of a desire to inspire others who may be walking a similar path of solitude and self-reliance. It is a book about the tenacity of the human spirit, the power of self-love, and the potential of embracing zone's true self.

Through my words, I hope to offer hope to those who feel lost, alone, and disconnected from the world around them. I hope to remind them that they are not defined by their solitude, their struggles, or their past, but by the strength, courage which lies within them. I hope to inspire them to clap for themselves, to celebrate their worth, their uniqueness, and their journey towards self-acceptance and self-empowerment.

So, as I finish this chapter of my life and look towards the horizon of new beginnings, I am filled with gratitude for the lessons learned, the challenges I overcame, and the connections created along the way. I am grateful for the solitude that shaped me, the loneliness that tested me, and the love that transformed me. And as I continue to walk this path of self-discovery and personal growth, I do so with a new sense of purpose, a deepened appreciation for the beauty of human connection, and a heart that beats with the rhythm of determination and continued faith in the power of the human spirit to rise above adversity.

——

I hope this book resonates with you and inspires you to love and accept your true self, connect with others, and celebrate your worth and uniqueness. If you ever feel lost or alone, remember that you are not defined by your circumstances but by the strength and courage that lies within you. Keep clapping for yourself, keep celebrating your journey, and keep shining your light brightly for the world to see.

Don't miss out!

Visit the website below and you can sign up to receive emails whenever Katie Rose publishes a new book. There's no charge and no obligation.

https://books2read.com/r/B-A-TUJAB-INFED

BOOKS2READ

Connecting independent readers to independent writers.

Also by Katie Rose

Starlight and Stilettos
The Butterfly Phoenix Project:
Chaos in the Kitchen
Moonbeam Chronicles: Witching Hour in Foxglove
When No One is Clapping for You, You Must Clap for Yourself

Watch for more at https://lovemymysticallife.com/.

About the Author

Raised in West Texas, Katie is a beacon of compassion, resilience, and empowerment. With 35 years of marriage under her belt, Katie now resides on a small rural farm in Georgia, where she has dedicated her life to rescuing unloved animals, inspiring older women to embrace their full potential, and expressing her creativity through the written word.

From a young age, Katie developed a deep connection with animals. Growing up in the Texas countryside, she witnessed the plight of abandoned and mistreated creatures, igniting a lifelong commitment to animal welfare. Now, on her small rural farm in Georgia, Katie has created a sanctuary where neglected animals find solace, healing, and a loving forever home.

Katie's passion for empowering older women stems from her belief that age should never be a barrier to personal growth and fulfillment. Through workshops, speaking engagements, and one-on-one coaching, she guides women on a transformative journey of self-discovery. Her unwavering support and encouragement inspire older women to embrace their unique strengths, unlock their hidden potential, and embark on new adventures with confidence and purpose. *

In addition to her dedication to animal rescue and empowering older women, Katie finds solace and self-expression through writing. Her words flow effortlessly onto the page, capturing the essence of her experiences, insights, and the beauty she witnesses in the world around her. Through her writing, Katie aims to inspire others to embrace their passions, live authentically, and make a positive impact in their own lives and the lives of others.

Katie's life is a testament to the power of compassion, resilience, and the pursuit of one's passions. Through her unwavering commitment to rescuing unloved animals, empowering older women, and expressing her creativity through writing, she has become a guiding light for all who cross her path.

Her journey serves as an inspiration to embrace our true selves, live with purpose, and make a positive impact in the world, regardless of age or circumstance.

Read more at https://lovemymysticallife.com/.